YOUR KNOWLEDGE HAS VALUE

- We will publish your bachelor's and master's thesis, essays and papers

- Your own eBook and book - sold worldwide in all relevant shops

- Earn money with each sale

Upload your text at www.GRIN.com
and publish for free

Bibliographic information published by the German National Library:

The German National Library lists this publication in the National Bibliography; detailed bibliographic data are available on the Internet at http://dnb.dnb.de .

This book is copyright material and must not be copied, reproduced, transferred, distributed, leased, licensed or publicly performed or used in any way except as specifically permitted in writing by the publishers, as allowed under the terms and conditions under which it was purchased or as strictly permitted by applicable copyright law. Any unauthorized distribution or use of this text may be a direct infringement of the author s and publisher s rights and those responsible may be liable in law accordingly.

Imprint:

Copyright © 2019 GRIN Verlag
Print and binding: Books on Demand GmbH, Norderstedt Germany
ISBN: 9783668928947

This book at GRIN:

https://www.grin.com/document/463630

Haitham Ismail

Protecting PII (Personal Identifiable Information) & PHI (Protected Health Information)

How to protect (PII) and (PHI)?

GRIN Verlag

GRIN - Your knowledge has value

Since its foundation in 1998, GRIN has specialized in publishing academic texts by students, college teachers and other academics as e-book and printed book. The website www.grin.com is an ideal platform for presenting term papers, final papers, scientific essays, dissertations and specialist books.

Visit us on the internet:

http://www.grin.com/

http://www.facebook.com/grincom

http://www.twitter.com/grin_com

PHI & PII Protection

How to protect (PII) and (PHI)?

Submitted by (Haitham Ismail)

How to protect (PII) and (PHI)?

Contents

PHI & PII Protection 0

    Contents 1

    List of tables 2

    Abstract. 3

    Introduction 3

    Policies, Procedures and Proper Documentation. 4

        Policies and Procedures 4

        Other documentation required 5

    Awareness, Training, and Education 5

    Security Controls 6

    Incident Response Plan 7

    Audits 8

    Author Recommendations 8

    References 10

How to protect (PII) and (PHI)?

List of tables

Table 1 - Policies Important for protecting PII & PHI 5

Table 2 – examples of Security Controls List.. 7

Table 3 - Benefits of being ISO Certified 8

Table 4 - General Author's recommendation 9

How to protect (PII) and (PHI)?

Abstract.

PII is Personal Identifiable Information is the information that can be used on its own or with other information to identify, contact, or locate a single person and it is maintained by the information technology department of any organization. An example of PII is data like names, place or date of birth, email address, National ID, Passport Number, employment information finical or medical records, etc. Likewise, PHI has Protected health information according to HIPA is any health information whether oral or recorded in any form of media which is created or received by a health care provider, public health authority, employer, life insurer or hospital. PII and PHI are different from any kind of data as it should be collected, maintained and disseminated according to fair information practice which is the base of Laws and regulations. In this article, we will discuss what is needed to make your organization able to handle securely and according to privacy laws. Furthermore, it will help in understanding the basic concepts of industry standards like HIPAA Security rule.

Introduction

McCallister et al. (2010) state in the NIST publications that organizations should maintain personal identification information (PII) data in all its stages within the organizations (e.g. collecting, maintaining and destructing) according to Fair Information Practices (Privacy Principles). The difference between PII data and other types of data that it should be not only protected but their treatment should be according to privacy law in the nation. For example, Fair Information Practices are the building blocks to the privacy laws in US. The fair information practice was established by Organizations of Economic Co-operations and Developments (OECD) and it includes principle like a limitation of the collection, limitation

How to protect (PII) and (PHI)?

use, data quality, etc. On the other hand, protected healthcare information (PHI) is health-related information that is treated by any entity in the healthcare industry. Scholl et al. (2008) state that an organization must show due care and due diligence in protecting PHI. Health Insurance Portability and Accountability Act (HIPAA) Security rule is a law that provides data privacy and security to medical and health information (Rouse, 2019). HIPPA main goal is to ensure confidentiality, integrity and availability of the PHI. Furthermore, it protects PHI against not permitted use or disclosure of PHI (Scholl et al, 2008). According to NIST, PHI and PII level of protection are determined with respect to their confidentiality Impact level. These impact levels are low, moderate and high which are determined based on the potential harm that could result to the subject individuals and/or the organization if PII or PHI were inappropriately accessed, used, or disclosed.

Due care and Due diligence will be proved in protecting PII and PHI by ensuring the implementations, operations and monitoring the following:

- Policies, Procedures and Documentation.
- Awareness, training and educations
- Technical security controls
- Incidence response
- Audits

Policies, Procedures and Proper Documentation.

Policies and Procedures

Organizations should develop, implement, maintain and monitor comprehensive policies and procedure for handling PII and PHI in the organization level, Program or component level and system level (McCallister et al., 2010; Scholl et al, 2008). Below is a sample of policies that are used to protect PHI and PII and its role.

How to protect (PII) and (PHI)?

Name	Comments
IT Security Incident Reporting and response policy	Describe How we handle data breaches (Tactical Monitoring initiative can help us to establish the program and write the policy)
Data Encryption Policy	For Mobile device or in transit of our network
	It should Indicate what should be encrypted,
	The encryption algorithm, Hashing Algorithm,
Vulnerability Management Policy	Guide us in assessing and hardening our servers, application (Securing access and storing)
Data Destruction policy	Guide us destructing data stored on a different kind of media
Access control policy	Guide us for establishing the AAA concept when Accessing data, and ensure accountability (Audits and logging)
Fraud, Waste, and Abuse Reporting Policy	Describe how Individual claiming possible fraud are reported and handled
System development security policy	Guide system developers to take security into consideration when they designing features in their backlogs.
Medical Information Collection Policy	Which describe how Bupa Arabia will collect, disclose, share and use PII & PHI

Table 1 - Policies Important for protecting PII & PHI

Other documentation required.

Security Baseline is an example of documents that works as a guide in implementing the minimum level of security on the related subject or technology (Livingston, 2000). For example, the baseline for Systems that are involved with PHI & PII handling (e.g. Server and PC) should be established, followed.

Examples.

- Security Baseline for PC and Laptop that are required to access the PHI & PII.
- Security Baseline for Servers (e.g. Active Directory, Exchange mailbox, SQL Server, etc.)

The benefits of having these documents are to have a minimum level of test security controls applied to the server and clients sides. These documents support the Information Security Policy and administrators and users are forced to follow it when handling PHI & PII.

Awareness, Training, and Education

NIST has guidelines for the establishment of the Information Technology Security Awareness and Training Program (NIST 800-50). It should be focused on the attention on the protection of PII and PHI. Different staff across Organizations should have periodic evaluated awareness campaigns methods which include:

How to protect (PII) and (PHI)?

- New scams that are used to steal identities.
- Providing updates on privacy items in the news (e.g. government data breach and their impact on the individual).
- How staff members are accountable for inappropriate actions with examples ☐ recommended good privacy practice.
- PII definition, How to handle it? And Retention schedule.

The goal is to build Knowledge and skills that enable Organizations IT departments to protect PII and PHI (Wilson and Hash, 2003).

Security Controls

These kinds of controls are required to protect the confidentiality of PII and PHI. Most of the known NIST Publication (800 - 53). This Publication enables the minimum required controls to protect information systems that are handling sensitive information (e.g. PII & PHI) that handle information in rest or in motion. This controls might be technical or administrative or physicals NIST SP (800-53) provides a catalogue of privacy and security controls, besides, continues organizational risk assessments (See Table 2, Page 7) that will help in selection and improvement of these controls (Joint Task Force, 2017). In the following tables, we will list examples of these controls that are mandatory to prove due care and due diligence.

How to protect (PII) and (PHI)?

Control Name	Comments
Enforcement Accesses controls	Policies (Through Firewalls), role-based access control (based on users), access PII & PHI through applications only, Encrypting PII & PHI data through NIST certified cryptographic algorithms
Separation of Duties	Enforce separation of duties for duties involving access to PII & PHI
Least Privilege	Apply the most restrictive rights/privileges to accesses PII & PHI
Remote Access	Strictly limit Access to PII & PHI from remote places from Mobile devices
Auditable Events	Monitor events that affect the confidentiality of PII & PHI
Identification and authentication	Level of authentication depending on the level of impact level
Media Access	Restrict media access to information System that includes PII & PHI (CD, USB, backup tapes)
Media Storage	Both in paper and digital forms until the media are destroyed (use storage encryption)
Media Transports	Encrypt PII & PHI when transmitting through the network (IPsec, HTTPS)
PII & PHI protection at rest	Protect PII & PHI on secondary storage (tapes)
Information System Monitoring	Uses Network Mentoring programs, syslog servers analyzers, SIM solutions
Vulnerability management	Continually Assessing PII & PHI systems for Hardening against new threats

Table 2 – examples of Security Controls List

Incident Response Plan

Organizations must develop IT Security Incident reporting response (See Table 1, page 5). It will asset organization in risk mitigation by guiding them in responding effectively and efficiently incidents. By implementing these plan, due care and due diligence will be shown by which incidents will be identified, analyzed, prioritized and handled (Cichonski et al, 2012). According to incident response, IT departments should create an Incident team internally or externally outsourced (e.g. Dell SecureWorks, EY, etc.).

How to protect (PII) and (PHI)?

Audits

It is important to go on different kind of periodical audits to assess all aspect of PII and PHI information systems. This audit will grantees assessing risks, reviewing threats, and enacting controls. Besides, it is considered as a first step in achieving industry standards compliance (Walsh, 2019). It is suggested to have as follows:

- Semi-annually audit (Internal Audit)
- Annually External audit

Author Recommendations

It is recommended to comply with the security industry standard (e.g. ISO 27001:2013, PCI, etc.). It serves as a guide for managing information in a secure manner by implementing all the practice and controls (technical or administrative or physical) are on the right track (See Table 3, Page 8). The benefits of being certified against industry standards can be summarized as follows:

Benefits	Comments
Marketing Edge	In a market which is more and more competitive, it is sometimes very difficult to find something that will differentiate you in the eyes of the organization's customers. ISO 27001 could be indeed a unique selling point, especially if you handle clients' sensitive information
Lowering Expenses	It lowers the operation cost by decreasing the cost of incidents.
Putting business in order	It helps in setting long and short term plans for information security. It set priority for the controls to be implemented in security.

Table 3 - Benefits of being ISO Certified

On the other hand, there is another recommendation can be followed when protecting PII and PHI that are collected based on experiences gained from working in the field.

How to protect (PII) and (PHI)?

Recommendation	Comments
Fully understand to complete the business process.	It is very important for the IT department candidates to understand the business process and objectives. This is will help them to understand the value of the information asset and how to protect them. This is can be achieved through strong orientation sessions for the new joiners.
Periodic Background check	All industry standards recommend background check for the new joiners. However, it is better to conduct a periodic background check (e.g. Annual background check). This will monitor the commitment and loyalty of the current employees and new Joiners as well.
Effective – Anti-Malware Solution	Use different types of AV. For example, Normal AV are signature based, which means it is detecting the virus based on a predefined. Other types depend on the reputation of the file. Therefore, an unknown reputation will not be executed. This will have protection over the zero-day attack. Vendors might have both types in one solution (e.g. McAfee ENS)
Sandboxing /Honeypots technologies	These techniques are used to allow hackers/Malware to be in a contained environment to detect their actions (Long, 2016). This will also help in detecting zero day's attacks. It can be on the cloud or on promises.
Integration	Better Incident response capability requires integrations between all controls. It enables sharing information and functions about threats and attacks among security solution to have better visibility over attack campaigns. For examples, integrations between Email gateways and Sandboxing technology enable protection from zero-day malware that might be attached in emails. Furthermore, it will share the information about this malware with endpoints for better protection against this newly seen malware.
Harden the infrastructure	System hardening means reaching the minimum level of the security vulnerability on a system (Scarfone et al., 2008). For example, 1. Install all patches of the operating systems and applications. 2. Disable unnecessary services (e.g. SNMP if not used). 3. Change the default setting (e.g. change the default password of admin or root accounts).
Add Security to change approval workflow	Security Approval should be mandatory when approving any change.

Table 4 - General Author's recommendation

References

JOINT TASK FORCE, 2017. Security and Privacy Controls for Information Systems and Organizations (NIST SP 800-53), [Online], Gaithersburg: U.S. Department of Commerce, Available at: https://csrc.nist.gov/CSRC/media//Publications/sp/800-53/rev-5/draft/documents/sp800-53r5-draft.pdf [Accessed 13 March 2019].

Livingston, G., 2000. How to Develop Your Company's First Security Baseline. [Online] Available at: https://www.giac.org/paper/gsec/170/develop-companys-first-security-baseline-standard/100648 [Accessed 13 March 2019].

Long, D., 2016. Deception and sandboxing. [Online] Available at: https://securingtomorrow.mcafee.com/business/deception-and-sandboxing/ [Accessed 20 March 2019].

McCallister, E. Grance, T. Scarfone, K. 2010. Guide to Protecting the Confidentiality of Personally Identifiable Information (PII) (NIST SP 800-122), [Online], Gaithersburg: U.S. Department of Commerce, Available at: https://nvlpubs.nist.gov/nistpubs/legacy/sp/nistspecialpublication800-122.pdf [Accessed 16 June 2017].

Cichonski, P., Millar, T., Grance, T., Scarfone, K., 2012. Computer Security Incident Handling Guide (NIST SP 800-61), [Online], Gaithersburg: U.S. Department of Commerce, Available at: https://nvlpubs.nist.gov/nistpubs/specialpublications/nist.sp.800-61r2.pdf [Accessed 12 March 2019].

Rouse, M., 2019. HIPAA (Health Insurance Portability and Accountability Act). [Online] Available at: https://searchhealthit.techtarget.com/definition/HIPAA [Accessed 12 March 2019].

Scarfone, K., Jansen,.W, Tracy, M. 2008. Guide to General Server Security (NIST SP 800-123)), [Online], Gaithersburg: U.S. Department of Commerce, Available at: https://nvlpubs.nist.gov/nistpubs/Legacy/SP/nistspecialpublication800-123.pdf [Accessed at 20 March 2019].

Scholl, M., Stine, K., Hash, J., Bowen, P., Johnson, A., Smith, C., and Steinberg, D. 2008. An Introductory Resource Guide for Implementing the Health Insurance Portability and Accountability Act (HIPAA) Security Rule (NIST SP 800-66r1), [Online], Gaithersburg: U.S. Department of Commerce, Available at: https://nvlpubs.nist.gov/nistpubs/Legacy/SP/nistspecialpublication800-66r1.pdf [Accessed 12 March 2019].

Walsh, K., 2019. What is Continuous Auditing? [Online] Available at: https://reciprocitylabs.com/what-is-continuous-auditing/ [Accessed 16 March 2019].

Wilson, M. and Hash, J. 2003. Building an Information Technology Security Awareness and Training Program (NIST SP 800-50), [Online], Gaithersburg: U.S. Department of Commerce, Available at: https://nvlpubs.nist.gov/nistpubs/legacy/sp/nistspecialpublication800-50.pdf [Accessed 13 March 2019].

YOUR KNOWLEDGE HAS VALUE

- We will publish your bachelor's and master's thesis, essays and papers

- Your own eBook and book - sold worldwide in all relevant shops

- Earn money with each sale

Upload your text at www.GRIN.com
and publish for free